D1238435

True Survival

STEVEN CALLAHAN

# ADRIFT IN THE ATLANTIC

Virginia Loh-Hagan

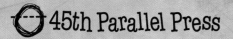 **45th Parallel Press**

Published in the United States of America by Cherry Lake Publishing
Ann Arbor, Michigan
www.cherrylakepublishing.com

Reading Adviser: Marla Conn MS, Ed., Literacy specialist, Read-Ability, Inc.
Book Designer: Felicia Macheske

Photo Credits: © DigtialStorm/iStock.com, cover; © MarcelClemens/Shutterstock.com, 5; © Goncalo Veloso de Figueiredo/Shutterstock.com, 7; © Dudarev Mikhail/Shutterstock.com, 8; © anyaivanova/Shutterstock.com, 11; © David Porras/Shutterstock.com, 12; © Ethan Daniels/Shutterstock.com, 14; © tonton/Shutterstock.com, 17; © WEI LING CHANG/Shutterstock.com, 19; © kim7/Shutterstock.com, 20; © Punchita Aisuriyasomporn/ Shutterstock.com, 23; © Anna Jurkovska/Shutterstock.com, 24; © VILevi/Shutterstock.com, 27; © Willyam Bradberry/Shutterstock.com, 29

Graphic Elements Throughout: © Gordan/Shutterstock.com; © adike/Shutterstock.com; © Yure/Shutterstock.com

**45th Parallel Press** is an imprint of Cherry Lake Publishing.

Library of Congress Cataloging-in-Publication Data

Names: Loh-Hagan, Virginia, author.
Title: Steven Callahan : adrift in the Atlantic / by Virginia Loh-Hagan.
Description: Ann Arbor, Michigan : Cherry Lake Publishing, 2018. | Series:
 True survival | Includes bibliographical references and index. | Audience:
 Grade 4 to 6.
Identifiers: LCCN 2017033501| ISBN 9781534107755 (hardcover) | ISBN
 9781534109735 (pdf) | ISBN 9781534108745 (pbk.) | ISBN 9781534120723
 (hosted ebook)
Subjects: LCSH: Callahan, Steven—Juvenile literature. | Napoleon Solo
 (Yacht)—Juvenile literature. | Shipwreck survival—Juvenile literature. |
 North Atlantic Ocean—Juvenile literature.
Classification: LCC G530.C24 L64 2018 | DDC 910.9163/1—dc23
LC record available at https://lccn.loc.gov/2017033501

Cherry Lake Publishing would like to acknowledge the work of The Partnership for 21st Century Skills.
Please visit *www.p21.org* for more information.

Printed in the United States of America
Corporate Graphics

# table of contents

# chapter one

# Smooth Sailing

## Who is Steve Callahan? How did he become a sailor? What is his dream?

Steve Callahan was born in 1952. He was born in Massachusetts. He lived by woods. He lived near a pond. He made little boats. He was a Boy Scout. His leader took him sailing. He learned a lot from him.

He read *Sailing Alone Around the World* by Joshua Slocum. Slocum was the first man to sail around the world by himself. He also read *Tinkerbelle* by Robert Manry. Manry sailed the shortest boat across the Atlantic. These two books inspired Callahan. Callahan dreamed of sailing across the Atlantic. He was 12 years old. He said, "Sailing feels right to me."

Callahan also loved learning about space.

# spotlight biography

In 2009, a Thai fishing boat carried 20 people. The boat broke. It sank. Most of the crew went overboard. No one saw them again. But two Burmese men grabbed on to a large icebox. The icebox was used to store fish. The men climbed into the icebox. There was a bad storm. There were heavy winds. There were heavy rains. There were sharks. The men stayed in the icebox. They drifted for 25 days. They drank rainwater. They ate old fish that was stuck in the icebox. A search plane found them. A helicopter came to get them. They were taken to hospitals. Then they went home. They were the only survivors of the accident.

Callahan went to the university. He studied **philosophy**. Philosophy is the study of thinking. It's the study of knowledge.

Callahan was more interested in boats. He said, "I love boats. And I've spent all my life around them." He designs boats. He builds boats. He teaches others about boats. He's an expert sailor. He races boats. He lives on boats. He writes about boats. Boats are his life.

He built a special boat. He named it the *Napoleon Solo*. The boat was just over 21 feet (6.4 meters). He built it by hand.

Callahan taught himself how to read the stars. This helps him find his way.

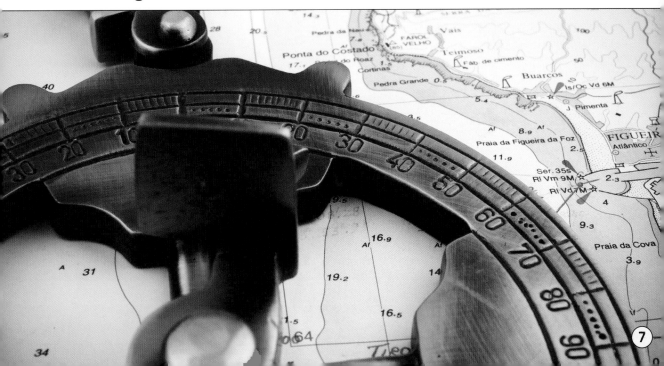

Callahan got married. He was married for 6 years. Then things changed. Their marriage ended. Callahan became sad. He needed to do something to make himself happy. He decided to make his dream come true.

He wanted to sail the *Napoleon Solo*. He wanted to sail alone. He wanted to sail across the Atlantic Ocean. He wanted to be like Slocum and Manry.

He was 29 years old. He set sail in 1981. He left Newport, Rhode Island. He sailed to Bermuda. He continued on to England. His trip across the Atlantic went smoothly. Smooth means without any problems.

◄ Callahan was inspired by his childhood heroes.

# chapter two

# Hole in the Boat

**Where did Callahan sail? How did his boat get damaged? What did he grab?**

Callahan left England. He headed to Antigua. He did this as part of a **solo** sailing race. Solo means alone. Callahan dropped out of the race. He was in Spain. Bad weather sunk several boats. The *Napoleon Solo* got damaged. Callahan fixed the boat. Then, he headed to the Canary Islands. He left the Canary Islands to go back home. He set sail on January 29, 1982.

The first 7 days were smooth. Then, he ran into trouble. He was in the middle of the Atlantic Ocean. One night there was a storm. He was sleeping. A loud crash woke him up. A whale may have hit him.

The Canary Islands are off the coast of Africa.

This happened at midnight. It was 2 days before his 30th birthday. His boat was badly damaged. There was a hole. Water gushed in.

Callahan said, "This is it. I'm going to die." Water flooded the boat. He said it felt like "someone had turned on 50 fire hoses."

He grabbed a knife. He got to the top of his boat. He had on a T-shirt. He had a special diving watch. He wore a whale's tooth necklace. That's all he wore for the next several months.

Callahan was below deck when the storm hit.

# explained by science

Lifeboats aren't used only in oceans. They're also in space. Trash floats around in space. It moves quickly. There are people inside the International Space Station. They get scared if trash heads toward them. Trash could damage the space station. If they were in danger, they'd get into a space lifeboat. They'd go back to Earth. Spacecraft designers have to think about two things. First, they need to think about power. Lifeboats need to be powered off when docked. But they still need to have air. They need something to move air around. Second, designers need to protect people from objects in space. Lifeboats need to take some hits. But they can't have a lot of heavy armor. They still need to be light.

His boat was sinking. He didn't panic. He dived into the cabin. He got survival things. The boat was flooding fast. He held his breath. He kept diving down. He kept getting stuff.

He grabbed a sleeping bag. He grabbed a floating **cushion**. Cushions are stuffed padding. He grabbed 3 pounds (1.4 kilograms) of food. He grabbed 8 pints (3.8 liters) of water. He grabbed maps. He grabbed an empty coffee can. He grabbed a spear gun. He grabbed **flares**. Flares give bursts of light. He grabbed **solar stills**. They turn seawater into drinking water. He grabbed a copy of *Sea Survival* by Dougal Robertson.

◄ Strong swimming skills helped save Callahan's life.

# chapter three

# Lost at Sea

**How did Callahan survive in his lifeboat?**
**How did Callahan feed himself?**

Callahan had enough supplies to last him 18 days. He threw everything in his lifeboat. His lifeboat was a blow-up raft. It was shaped like a circle. It was 6 feet (2 m) across.

There was a big wave. It pushed the lifeboat away from the *Napoleon Solo*. Waves beat the sides of his lifeboat. Callahan used the coffee can to scoop out water. He **drifted**. Drift means to float away. He said, "I knew I was totally alone."

He was in the middle of the ocean. He signaled for help. Rescue planes couldn't hear him. Ships couldn't see him. Callahan had to save himself.

Callahan saw nine ships.

# would you?

- **Would you throw others out of a lifeboat?** Lifeboats only hold so many people. *William Brown* was an American ship. It hit an iceberg. It sank in 1841. People got on a lifeboat. The lifeboat was sinking. Survivors kicked out 16 people. They did this to save their own lives.

- **Would you abandon ship?** Abandoning ship means jumping into the ocean. A basic rule of sea survival is "Your ship is the best lifeboat." Stay on the ship as long as you can.

- **Would you eat raw fish?** It's always risky to eat raw meat. But raw fish is the least risky. It has the least amount of bad germs. Still, people should be careful. Make sure the fish is fresh.

He named his lifeboat *Rubber Ducky*. **Barnacles** collected on the bottom. Barnacles are little sea animals. They look like white rocks. Small fish ate the barnacles. Big fish ate the little fish. Soon, fish surrounded Callahan.

He learned "to live like an **aquatic** caveman." Aquatic means water. He ate barnacles. He ate birds. But he mostly ate fish. He speared fish. There was no way for him to make fire. He ate them raw. He ate the organs first. He dried fish meat to eat later. He dried it in the sun.

Dried fish helped keep Callahan alive.

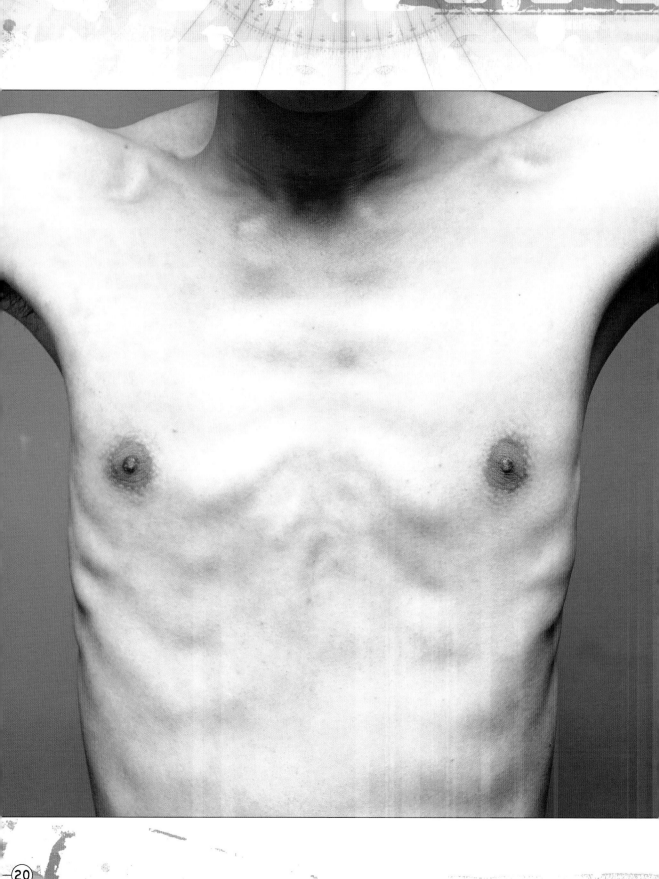

Callahan was sad. He was in pain. Around day 40, he speared a fish. The fish fought back. It ripped a hole in his lifeboat. His lifeboat was leaking air. Sharks circled him. Callahan had to stay afloat. He fixed the hole. But the hole kept opening. Finally, he patched the hole with fishing line and a fork. It took him 10 days to fix his lifeboat.

On day 74, he had three cans of water left. His body and mind were shutting down. He was about to give up.

◄ Callahan drifted for 1,800 nautical miles (3,334 km) across the ocean. He had little food and water.

# chapter four

# Fish to the Rescue!

**How did the fish save him? How was he rescued?**

Fish kept Callahan company. They were his food. And they saved him.

On day 76, fishermen came. They saw birds flying over the lifeboat. The birds were hunting fish. The fish were following Callahan. The fishermen came to find fish. They also found Callahan. They normally wouldn't fish in that area.

They were surprised to find him. Callahan had lost 40 pounds (18 kg). He had a lot of sores. He was sunburned.

The fishermen asked Callahan what he was doing. Callahan was so happy. He said, "Everything was beautiful."

Birds led the fishermen to the fish—and Callahan.

Callahan was rescued, but all his fish were caught.

He told the fishermen to finish fishing. He said, "They work hard for a dollar down there." The fishermen fished for 2 hours. They caught all of Callahan's fish.

Callahan was on their boat. The dead fish lay all around him. He said, "They had come 1,800 miles with me, saved my life, and now they were being rewarded with death and the fish market. That's the sea for you."

Callahan finally saw land. He was by Marie-Galante. This is an island in the Caribbean. Callahan was saved on April 21, 1982.

# survival tips

## LOST AT SEA!

- Collect fresh water. Catch and store rainwater. Use plastic bags as containers. Never drink ocean water.

- Let rain soak your clothes. Squeeze water out to drink.

- Rinse containers with the first raindrops. This washes away salt. Use this water to clean cuts. Use this water to clean food.

- Keep your clothes on. It's easy to get sunburned in an open boat.

- Don't get rid of clothes. Layer up at night. It gets cold. Use clothes as shade during the day.

- Look for planes and ships. Use a mirror or phone screen to reflect sunlight. This can be seen up to 10 miles (16 kilometers) away on a sunny day.

- Plug leaks. Use duct tape.

# chapter five

# Landed!

## What happened to Callahan when he got to land? How did Callahan live after surviving?

Callahan had told himself he was a sea creature. But he learned he could never live at sea. He said, "I very much needed people."

He was excited to get to shore. But he couldn't stand up. He was weak. His feet had swelled up. His legs were cramped. When he got to land, he fell. He couldn't walk for 6 weeks. His legs had to get used to walking again.

He was taken to a hospital. He left that night. He stayed on the island. He healed. Then he spent time on different boats.

Callahan only spent one day in the hospital.

# Rest in Peace

Caitriona Lucas was from Ireland. She had a husband. She had 2 children. She was 41 years old. She was a librarian. She also helped the Coast Guard. She was a search-and-rescue volunteer. In 2016, Lucas went to get the body of a missing man. She went with two other people. She was in a raft. There were big waves. The raft turned over. It crashed by cliffs. Lucas was thrown into the ocean. She passed out. A helicopter picked her up. Doctors tried to help. She died. She's the first member of the Irish Coast Guard to die on duty. Her son said, "Good-bye to our wonderful mother. Love always. You are my hero."

Callahan still likes sailing. He went on many more sailing trips. He crossed the ocean several times. He wasn't scared. He respected the ocean.

He invented better lifeboats. He became an expert on shipwrecks. He became an expert on sea survival. He wrote books about his survival. He spoke about it. He was on TV.

He still remembers his hard times. He always has peanut butter with him. He saves water. He has to make himself drink.

At 30, he fought for his life at sea. At 60, he fought for his life against **cancer**. Cancer is a sickness. He is a fighter.

Callahan said the sea is "the world's greatest wilderness."

# Did You Know?

- *Life of Pi* is a movie. It was made in 2012. Ang Lee was the director. He hired Callahan. He wanted Callahan to share what life was like on a lifeboat. Callahan made some of the tools seen in the movie.

- Callahan wrote while sailing the *Napoleon Solo*. He wrote stories. He wrote letters. He scribbled pictures of sea monsters in bow ties.

- There was a camera attached to the back of the *Napoleon Solo*. The camera took pictures of storms. The pictures were lost with the boat.

- Callahan saw a whale and her baby breach close to him. The whales were 100 feet (30.5 m) away.

- Callahan grew close to his fish. He called them his "little doggies."

- Sharks rubbed themselves against his lifeboat. One hammerhead shark liked to play with the lifeboat's tubes.

- Callahan broke one of his solar stills. He did this on purpose. He wanted to learn how solar stills work.

- Callahan had food for a few weeks. He had 10 ounces (283.5 grams) of peanuts. He had 16 ounces (453.5 g) of baked beans. He had a box of eggs. He had two cabbages. He had 10 ounces of corned beef. He had 10 ounces of raisins. Most of his food was soaked by seawater.

- Callahan said, "To this day, I feel enlightened by what I went through because it changed me for the better. But would I want to be adrift in the ocean again? No way!"

# Consider This!

**Take a Position:** Do you think people should be allowed to sail by themselves? What are the benefits of sailing alone? What are the risks of sailing alone? Argue your point with reasons and evidence.

**Say What?** Callahan grabbed what he could. Pretend that you're adrift at sea. If you could only bring five items, what would they be? Describe each item. Explain your reasoning for each item.

**Think About It!** Callahan said, "Nobody ever invented anything or discovered anything without taking some risk and embarking on some kind of adventure." What do you think about this statement? Invent something. Think about the risks. Think about the adventures.

# Learn More

- Callahan, Steven. *Adrift: Seventy-Six Days Lost At Sea*. Boston: Houghton Mifflin, 2002.
- Cefrey, Holly. *Steven Callahan: Adrift At Sea*. New York: Children's Press, 2003.

# Glossary

**aquatic** (uh-KWAT-ik) of the water

**barnacles** (BAHR-nuh-kuhlz) sea animals that look like white rocks

**cancer** (KAN-sur) sickness

**cushion** (KUSH-uhn) stuffed padding

**drifted** (DRIFT-id) floated away

**flares** (FLAIRZ) tools that make bursts of light

**philosophy** (fuh-LAH-suh-fee) the study of thinking and knowledge

**solar stills** (SOH-lur STILZ) tools that turn seawater into drinking water

**solo** (SOH-loh) alone

# Index

# About the Author

Dr. Virginia Loh-Hagan is an author, university professor, former classroom teacher, and curriculum designer. She likes floating and reading in her pool. She can't imagine being stranded in the ocean for 76 days. She lives in San Diego with her very tall husband and very naughty dogs. To learn more about her, visit www.virginialoh.com.